S0-AQK-520

ANIMALS in DANGER

Leatherback Turtle

Rod Theodorou

Heinemann LIBRARY

H www.heinemann.co.uk

Visit our website to find out more information about **Heinemann Library** books.

To order:

☎ Phone 44 (0) 1865 888066

🖹 Send a fax to 44 (0) 1865 314091

🖥 Visit the Heinemann Bookshop at www.heinemann.co.uk to browse our catalogue and order online.

First published in Great Britain by Heinemann Library, Halley Court, Jordan Hill, Oxford OX2 8EJ, a division of Reed Educational and Professional Publishing Ltd.
Heinemann is a registered trademark of Reed Educational & Professional Publishing Limited.

OXFORD MELBOURNE AUCKLAND JOHANNESBURG BLANTYRE
GABORONE IBADAN PORTSMOUTH NH (USA) CHICAGO

© Reed Educational and Professional Publishing Ltd 2001
The moral right of the proprietor has been asserted.

Designed by Ron Kamen
Illustrations by Dewi Morris/Robert Sydenham
Originated by Ambassador Litho Ltd.
Printed and bound in Hong Kong/China

ISBN 0431 00140 5
05 04 03 02 01
10 9 8 7 6 5 4 3 2 1

British Library Cataloguing in Publication Data
Theodorou, Rod
　　Leatherback Turtle - (Animals in Danger)
　　1.Leatherback Turtle - Juvenile literature 2.Endangered species - Juvenile literature
　　I.Title
　　597.9'2

Acknowledgements
The Publishers would like to thank the following for permission to reproduce photographs: Ardea: p12, Francois Gohier p4, Masahiro Lijima pp16, 26; Bat Conservation International: Merlin D Tuttle p4; BBC: Lynn M Stone p4; Bruce Coleman: Gerald S Cubitt p20; FLPA: Fritz Polking p22; NHPA: Anthony Bannister p14, Peter Pickford p8, Jany Sauvanet p18; OSF: p13, David Cayless p24, Olivier Grunewald pp 9, 15, 19, 21, John Mitchell p27; Doug Perrine/Seapics: pp6, 7, 11; Still Pictures: p5, Pascal Kobeh p25; WWF Photolibrary: p17, Alain Compost p23.

Cover photograph reproduced with permission of Bruce Coleman: Gerald S Cubitt.

Our thanks to Henning Dräger at WWF-UK for his comments in the preparation of this book.

Every effort has been made to contact copyright holders of any material reproduced in this book. Any omissions will be rectified in subsequent printings if notice is given to the Publisher.

Contents

Any words appearing in the text in bold, **like this**, are explained in the Glossary.

Animals in danger

whooping
crane

grey bat

polar bear

All over the world, more than 25,000 animal
species are in danger. Some are in danger because
their home is being **destroyed**. Many are in
danger because people hunt them.

4

This book is about leatherback turtles and why they are in danger. Unless people learn to look after them, leatherback turtles will become **extinct**. We will only be able to find out about them from books like this.

What are leatherback turtles?

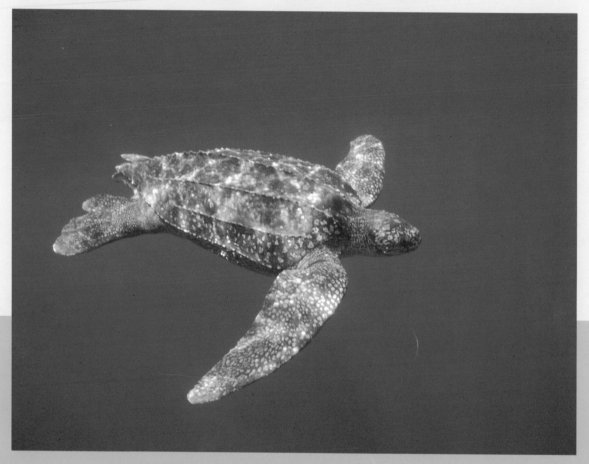

Leatherback turtles are **reptiles**. They are the largest **marine** turtles in the world. They travel further, and dive deeper, than any other turtle.

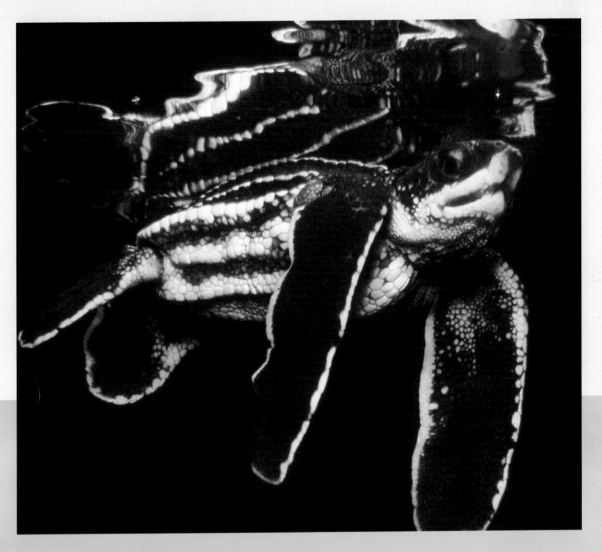

Marine turtles spend all their lives at sea. They have to come to the surface to breathe air. All marine turtles are **endangered** animals.

What do leatherback turtles look like?

Leatherback turtles have very large front flippers which make them strong swimmers. They have seven long ridges running down their shells.

Leatherbacks are named after their shells. All other turtles have hard shells. Leatherbacks have rubbery shells that feel a bit like wet **leather**.

Where do leatherback turtles live?

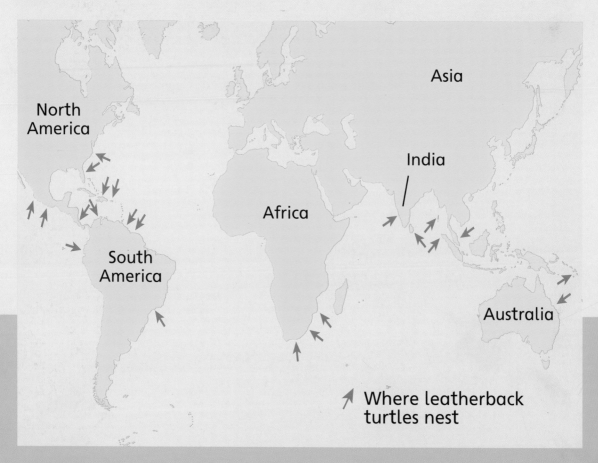

North America

Asia

India

Africa

South America

Australia

↗ Where leatherback turtles nest

Leatherbacks swim in all the warm waters of the world. They nest on the coasts of North America, South America, India and parts of Africa, Asia and Australia.

10

Leatherbacks are such strong swimmers that they can swim in the open ocean, a long way from land. All other **marine** turtles always swim close to the coasts.

What do leatherback turtles eat?

Leatherback turtles are **omnivores**. Their favourite food is **jellyfish**. They will also eat seaweed, **molluscs** and small fish.

Leatherbacks can eat twice their own body weight of jellyfish in one day! The jellyfish stings do not hurt them or make them ill.

Leatherback turtle babies

In spring, at night, **female** leatherbacks swim up to a sandy beach. They pull themselves out of the water and crawl up the beach. Then they dig a hole with their back flippers.

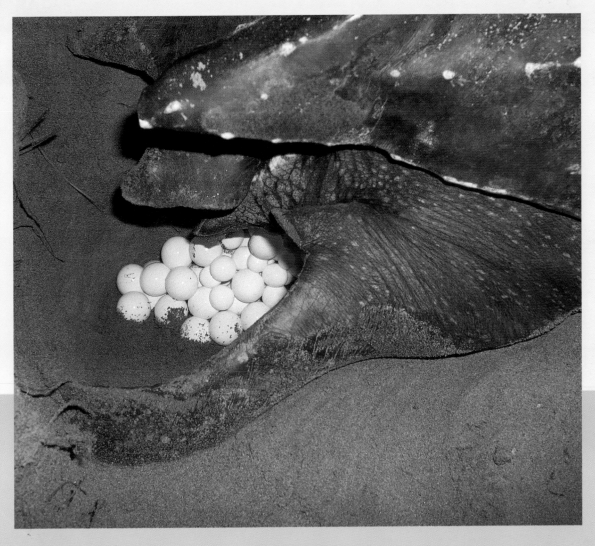

The females lay about 60 white eggs in the nest and then cover the eggs up with sand. The females return to the sea once more.

Race for the Sea

About two months later the eggs hatch. The tiny baby leatherbacks dig themselves out of the sand and crawl towards the sea.

Seabirds, crabs and other animals attack the baby turtles. In the water, sharks and other big fish snap them up. Many die, but many others escape and swim away.

Unusual leatherback turtle facts

After a **female** turtle has laid her eggs she returns to the sea. It may be two or three years before she touches land again, to lay more eggs. **Male**s spend all their lives in the sea.

Female leatherbacks can swim over 4000 kilometres from the beach where they laid their eggs. When it is time to lay more eggs they find their way back to exactly the same beach!

How many leatherback turtles are there?

It is very hard to count leatherbacks in the vast oceans, but we can count their nests. In 1992 a nest count showed there were about 70,000 **female** leatherbacks left alive.

We know the number of nests gets less every
year. Many beaches now have no nests at all.
There may be fewer than 39,000 female
leatherbacks left.

Why is the leatherback turtle in danger?

Leatherbacks like soft, gentle, sandy beaches to nest on. Sadly, these are also the beaches that people like. This is bad news for the turtles.

Beach chairs, boats and bright lights confuse and frighten the **female** turtles. People also steal their eggs and hunt them for food.

Why is the leatherback turtle in danger?

Many turtles are caught in the nets of fishermen who are **trawling** for **shrimp**. About 1500 turtles die every year in shrimp nets.

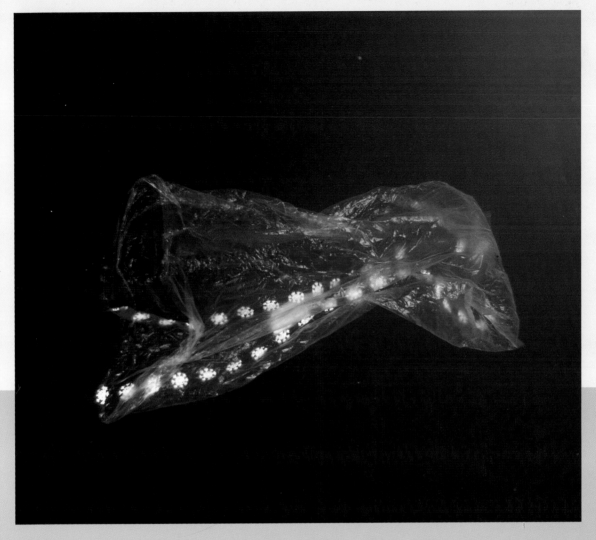

Sometimes leatherback turtles eat poisonous balls of **tar** from oil spills. Floating plastic bags and balloons look like jellyfish. When the turtles eat them they can die.

How is the leatherback turtle being helped?

Stealing turtle eggs is now illegal in most countries. Scientists and police **patrol** the beaches at night, but it is very hard to protect all the nests from egg thieves.

Sometimes scientists dig up the eggs and take them to a safe place to hatch. When they are ready they take the baby turtles to the sea at night. Then they let them go.

Leatherback turtle factfile

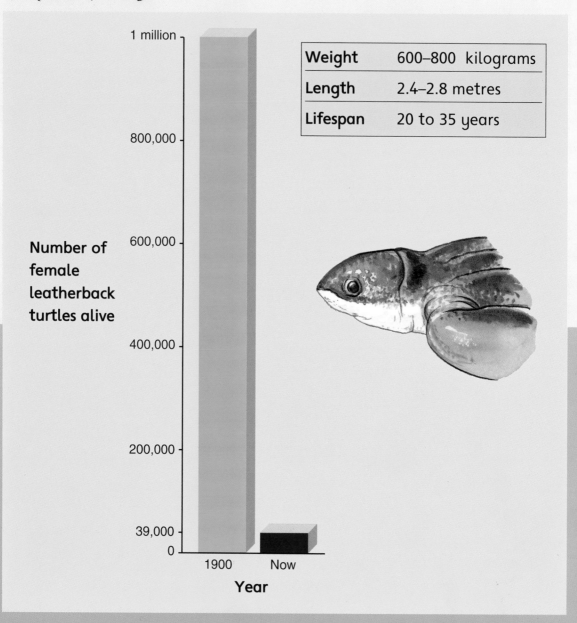

Weight	600–800 kilograms
Length	2.4–2.8 metres
Lifespan	20 to 35 years

Number of female leatherback turtles alive

Year

1900   Now

World danger table

	Number that may have been alive 100 years ago	Number that may be alive today
Cheetah	135,000	15,000
Grey bat	6.3 million	900,000
Koala	2 million	65,000
Polar bear	710,000	24,000
Whooping crane	2100	400

There are thousands of other animals in the world that are in danger of becoming **extinct**. This table shows some of these animals.

Can you find out more about them?

Further reading, addresses and websites

Books

Amazing Crocodiles and Reptiles, Amazing Worlds series, Mary Ling, Dorling Kindersley, 1991

A Step-by-step Book About Turtles, Johannes Jahn, TFH Publications, 1998

Find Out About Reptiles, Joyce Pope, Aladdin Books Ltd, 1985

Leatherback Turtle, Endangered Animals series, Sylvia Funston and Olena Kassian, Owl Communications, 1992

The Tortoise Trust Guide to Tortoises and Turtles, Andy Highfield, Krieger Publishing Company, 1998

Turtles and Tortoises, Hartmut Wilke, Barron's Education series, 1998

Organizations

Friends of the Earth: UK - 26–28 Underwood Street, London N1 7JQ ☎ (020) 7490 1555
Australia - 312 Smith Street, Collingwood, VIC 3065 ☎ 03 9419 8700

Greenpeace: UK - Canonbury Villas, London N1 2PN ☎ (020) 7865 8100
Australia - Level 4, 39 Liverpool Street, Sydney, NSW 2000 ☎ 02 9261 4666

WWF: UK - Panda House, Weyside Park, Catteshall Lane, Godalming, Surrey GU7 1XR ☎ (01483) 426444
Australia - Level 5, 725 George Street, Sydney, NSW 2000 ☎ 02 9281 5515

Useful websites

www.museum.gov.ns.ca
The Nova Scotia turtles site.

www.seaworld.org
The Sea World site has excellent photos and information about turtles.

www.turtles.org
This marine turtle conservation site contains photos and clear information about leatherback turtles.

www.wwf.org
WWF (World Wide Fund For Nature) is the world's largest independent conservation organization. WWF conserves wildlife and the natural environment for present and future generations.

Glossary

destroyed	spoilt, broken or torn apart so it can't be used
endangered	animals that are nearly extinct
extinct	dead and can never live again
female	girl or woman
jellyfish	animals that float in the sea and have bodies like jelly
leather	type of tough material made from the skin of animals
male	boy or man
marine	something that lives in the sea
mollusc	animal with a shell covering its body, like a snail
omnivore	an animal that eats plants and animals
patrol	to guard an area and keep watch
reptiles	snakes, lizards, crocodiles, turtles, tortoises and other animals that are cold-blooded and covered in scales
shrimp	small sea animal that has many legs and a shell around its body
species	a group of the same animals or plants
tar	sticky chemical made from oil
trawling	fishing with a large net shaped like a bag

Index

Titles in the *Animals in Danger* series include:

Hardback   0 431 00136 7

Hardback   0 431 00139 1

Hardback   0 431 00140 5

Hardback   0 431 00141 3

Hardback   0 431 00142 1

Hardback   0 431 00143 X

Find out about other Heinemann books on our website www.heinemann.co.uk/library